Tea and Talk

with Friends

Tea and Talk

with Friends

Photographs, Poetry, Prose
Prayers

Amy Pierson and Julie Stephens

Tea and Talk with Friends

© Copyright, 2011-2023
by Julie Stephens & Amy Pierson

Photographs by Julie Stephens
All rights reserved.
Hands Be Strong Publishing
handsbestrong.com

No part of this book may be used or reproduced in any manner whatsoever without written permission, except in the case of brief quotations embodied in critical articles or reviews.

All scripture quotations are from the King James Bible unless otherwise noted.

9 8 7 6 5 4 3

First Edition October 2011
Third Printing July 2023

Second Edition

ISBN: 978-0-9742680-6-4 (print)
ISBN: 978-1-7364304-2-2 (eBook)

Library of Congress Control Number: 2011917806

Welcome to *Tea and Talk*...

**Come,
Let us have some tea And
continue to talk About
happy things.**
Chaim Potok

Read what others are saying about *Tea and Talk*

I love the *Tea and Talk* theme! Your book reminds me of dear friends I have but don't see every year, and when I do, it is like we were never apart. These types of friendships are rare as described in your book. Your photos are uniquely special to the stories and poems, and give added meaning visually, as they relate. Thank you for sharing this with me.
Diana Waguespack
Bachelor of Science in Education, Art All Levels, Professional Photographer

I think it is beautiful!! I like the way you two have tied together the threads of your poetry, prose and photos. I think *Tea and Talk* will have a wide audience.
Phyllis Kayne, Published Poet and Artist

I really like *Tea and Talk*. It is a wonderful gift. I wish you luck with your book. It is a good idea.
Bob Stigall, Professional Photographer

Thank you for allowing me the opportunity to review part of your new book! I really like the concept and am looking forward to publication and subsequent placement in my store. I want this book in my shop because it will appeal to women and anyone with friendships in general.
I like that it is uplifting, and filled with Love. It touched my heart and soul when I read the first portion, so I know it will touch others as well. I broke into tears when I read the "bald" story by Amy, reminding me of my own bout with cancer, and the folks that support you through it. Excellent book! Light & Love,
Alice Attaway
Owner of Back Country Navigator

Tea and Talk is well written, interesting, a delightful read with beautiful photographs.
Bob Hines
Retired Creative Art Director and Artist

I've previewed the section of ***Tea and Talk*** that you sent me. I know you have not written this for male friends, especially ones like me with no feminine side. But, I have seen your photography and each picture speaks volumes for the place you are taking your reader's heart; whether it's an intimate walk in the woods or a storm coming in over the mountains, you bring your readers with you so they feel the rain and snow in their face, or the gentle sound of golden leaves falling in the forest. You are a blessing to all who know you. You live the life of a loving, caring person, and it shows in your writing. I'm pleased to call you friend.
      Chuck Chetwin
      Professional Nature Photographer

I loved reading the preview of your new book, ***Tea and Talk***. What a great idea! Special friends are rare, and this book will be a treasure for them. I love the way you put pictures in reader's minds as you tell the story. Your photographs are great; the poetry and ideas will touch hearts. There are heartwarming stories that I believe are needed at times like the world is having now. We need to hold on to the special people in our lives and your book will be a constant reminder of this. Good Luck. I'll buy a copy and more for special friends.
      Karen Hurd, Nature Artist and
      Author of *My Sweety – The heartbreak and joy of loving a wild mule deer.*

This lovely book offers a unique and charming concept of what makes life good. "A conversation that will never end" encompasses the meaning of friendship.
      Olyve Hallmark Abbott
      Author of four paranormal books and two novels.

Julie

The beginning of Amy and Julie

The beginning of closeness
Cannot be bounded up like stairs
Two at a time
It must be coaxed softly
Taking one tiny step
And then another
Lightly

    The inspiration for this poem, I call "The Beginning of Amy and Julie" came when my husband and I were at a turning point in our lives. Life was proving to be much different than we had planned. You don't always get what you want, right? As we were struggling to understand why and what we were to do, we were living in Colorado when our home in Texas was broken into. We had been robbed. I could hardly digest all that this meant. Just in from work, I was drained physically and emotionally. I had nothing left to give. I could not go with my husband to our weekly volunteer program.
    Alone for the first time all day, I was trying to decide if I would pour myself a glass of wine or two, telephone a friend, or go into the shower and wail, when there was a knock at the door.
    Amy had come by with my dishes. A couple of nights before I had taken dinner to the neighbors I did not know. I had heard that they had discovered a broken water pipe upon arriving home after an eighteen hour drive. Knowing what a draining, long drive feels like, I knew that fresh bread and homemade soup would be welcomed.

As not to return empty dishes, Amy had made a chocolate cake. I put on the tea kettle. We sat down and began a conversation that will never end.

Amy's daughter, Stephanie, was in treatment for breast cancer at that time. There was much on the heart of my friend-to-be.

I am seldom without my camera. I took this picture on an 'Amy and Julie adventure' and this photograph inspired that poem.

Amy

Traveling the two days from Texas to Colorado with a very sick child, four dogs, and two cats had its traumatic moments and had been exhausting. Our daughter, Stephanie, was suffering the effects of undergoing chemotherapy treatments for breast cancer. Her missing cat from the motel room, which we found two hours after the search began, had its emotional impact on all of us. Upon arrival at our mountain home, we discovered a leak that had to be repaired before we could reconnect the water.

It was a Sunday evening when my husband, Bob, and I were in town that a neighbor, we didn't know, brought homemade soup and freshly baked bread to our door. Stephanie was barely able to get up off the couch to accept this blessing. Several days later, I returned the dishes with some chocolate sheet cake and met this thoughtful neighbor. Julie had been upset and crying. After a few words at the door, she asked me to come in for a cup of tea. Over a cup of tea I learned that, not only had their home in Texas been broken into and items stolen, but that her mother had passed away two months prior from cancer. We connected that day, and a friendship began with **Tea and Talk**.

Julie

This book is the sharing of love, friendship, simple joys, and everyday pleasures. It is the sharing of what is important to us. It is conveying the feeling of being so excited about new cards I have created with my photographs and poetry, that I run over to show Amy, breathlessly climbing her stairs and calling her name, as a child delights in showing mother her latest artwork.

It is the excitement of being a first time grandma and sharing all that is inside of me with my girlfriend, Susie, who has also just become a first time grandma, even as I am unable to put words to all my feelings, she understands. Completely. The joys and the sorrows together are shared.

I told Susie that our son says they are coming for Thanksgiving! That means we get to see our baby grandson again soon! The next thing I know Susie has sent the softest, most endearing baby towel with a sweet note: "Julie and Bruce, one of my treasures is bathing our grandchild and wrapping her up for snuggles in a hooded towel. I can 'picture' you with Caleb at Thanksgiving." Love, Susie. My eyes water; I thank God for my girlfriend Susie.

It is emailing my daughter that getting up at 5:00 AM was totally worth it just to see the stars. I write, "The stars are dazzling ~ the Milky Way ~ the Big Dipper ~ Orion the Hunter ~ the sky is completely filled with stars! There is no more room!~
OMG...between rain, the full moon and being so sick, I hadn't seen the stars like this in so long~   I   even saw a shooting star ~ amazing ~ glorious ~ so humbling."

For as long as I can remember, nature, reading, writing, and photography have provided me with encouragement, coziness, and comfort. They have been a source of solace for me.

I had my Brownie camera at four or five years-old outside taking pictures of the sunlight coming through the trees and taking pictures of the other kids playing. I cannot remember not being able to read. Indeed, I eventually read Henry David Thoreau, Laura Ingalls Wilder, Alice Walker, Edna St. Vincent Millay, Joy Adamson, Madeleine L'Engle, Emily Dickinson, Ralph Waldo Emerson and many other writers who delighted in nature as I do.

I relish the balance that I find in both the solitude of nature and the communal gathering I enjoy with the 'tea and talk' of girlfriends; the joining of like-minded thinkers through reading and the oneness I am with my camera in nature.

Everything I love can be enjoyed both by myself and with those I love. I get great pleasure watching the stars alone, feeling God's presence, or in my husband's arms when we stargaze together. I am in bliss with my camera alone with a doe and her fawn, but I also can't wait to share the moment in time that I have captured with my girlfriend, Amy, or my husband or son or daughter.

To me all we really have in life besides this moment in time are our relationships and our memories. May we take the time to care for these blessings and for our earth. Nature is not just a pretty backdrop for our lives, but an integral, connected part of our lives to be respected, loved, and cared for. I hope this little volume encourages this attitude. – Written at the Cabin, Lake City, Colorado, Elevation 8865 ft.

Somewhere along life's journey every woman will ask herself, is there something else I can do besides the role I am in presently, how can I touch the world, or what new adventure is there for me to enjoy?

Thanks to a new daughter-in-law, I started quilting. She had thirty-year-old quilt tops from her Granny that she wanted put together. Never in my wildest dreams did I ever think I would quilt, let alone enjoy it. I have since designed my own patterns, and though I sew by the seat of my pants, so to speak, I have made beautiful quilts. Most importantly is the wonderful relationship that has developed with my daughter-in-law. See the story, "Angela's Quilt." In the future, I plan to write a documentary entitled, "Mom, I have Breast Cancer," which is my daughter's story of hope, courage, and survival.

Over the years, I have developed a positive attitude toward life and its challenges to me, so that I expect the best from every situation. I have reverence for all of life and thankfulness for all blessings. One of the talents God has given me is writing poetry. All of us want to be recognized, up lifted, encouraged, and appreciated. Through poetry, I can do these things.

This could not have been truer than when I experienced the difficulty of leaving all of my co-workers of more than twenty years. We were like family going through the ups and downs of the airline industry, and sharing our personal triumphs and tragedies. They lovingly called me "The Real Boss" since I pretty much ran the show, even though I was not the manager.

One of the first poems I wrote was a tribute to the employees, mentioning each and every one by name, those still present or retired, and it included those who had passed away. It eased my pain of leaving and gave them a few laughs. This was not the end, but a new beginning for each one of us.

My first poem published was "Happy Valentine's Day Dear Bob," a love note to my husband. Then, I was asked to contribute a poem for publication in "The International Who's Who in Poetry," one of 250 to be included. I sent my favorite poem, "The Happy Face." When the book arrived, there was a page in the front entitled, "Featured Poets." For the beginning of the book, they had chosen a diverse sampling of four poets and poetry from around the world. When I turned the page, I was the very first Poet featured, "The Happy Face" on the right page, and my Poets Profile on the left page. You cannot imagine how thrilled and humbled I was. This experience has inspired me to write the stories behind the poems. The dream to publish my own book of poetry is now coming to fruition with the collaboration of Julie on this book.

My hope for everyone who reads this book is that it will touch your heart, women meeting with women, to make you think, laugh, begin something new. Opportunities can be very subtle, so dare to dream and dare to win.

Stephanie is now a five year breast cancer survivor enjoying life to its fullest.

Written at the Lake House, Lake Winnsboro, Texas.

Julie

This summer morning my romantic husband brought me a colorful bouquet of wild flowers, as he frequently does. He was excited to explain that the wild flowers were blooming abundantly due to an underwater spring that kept the plant life vivid in this hot and dry time of the year.

In my bouquet this morning was a cluster of luminous pink and yellow lantana. This brought another smile to my eyes, as I remembered my great-grandmother calling these pink and yellow flowers that are so closely arranged together on the plant, 'ham and eggs.' Maw-Maw lived with Paw-Paw in Clermont Harbor, Mississippi, a little village now wiped away by Katrina that used to exist in the Gulfport area. For a moment I was a bit of a girl again and Maw-Maw and Paw-Paw were alive...such simple folk, living in nature and working by the sweat of their brow.

By the sweat of your brow
In the sweat of thy face shalt thou eat bread,
till thou return unto the ground;
for out of it wast thou taken: for dust thou art,
and unto dust shalt thou return.
Genesis 3:19

Maw-Maw and Paw-Paw's house, that Paw-Paw built, had a big, screened porch. By the time I could remember they were very old and would wait on the porch in rocking chairs for our arrivals and departures. The one bathroom had a big, claw-footed tub. Each room had key holes which were skeleton key locks that called out to be looked into.

The enormous whitewashed pecan trees off the back porch provided a shady place to play in the dirt. As sweat rolled down my face my earth-crusted fingers gave me smudges across my cheeks and nose. Still no matter how hot and thirsty I became, I couldn't make myself drink the water which smelled like rotten eggs.

Well, that was many years ago, and yet, I cannot forget such simple things in life, for it is the simple things in life that are important; remembering my great-grandparents, the charm and character of an old-fashioned house, people working by the sweat of their brow, living close to nature, and a husband bringing his beloved wife a bouquet of wildflowers.

A deeper hue than man can create
A robin's egg
A bit of grace

Flitting, dashing, scurrying, zipping, zooming
In search of the prefect flower
Not a bee but a bird
Superpower
Tiny thing
Love from above

21

Today is 9/11/11. This picture was taken last year when I visited my long time, dear girlfriend, Jules, at her home on Long Island.

Jules and I became friends when we were both living in Tulsa, Oklahoma. I was newly married and had badly burned my hand frying chicken for the first time. I ran across the street to my neighbor, and my friend took care of me.

Jules and her husband moved back 'home' to New York, and though we didn't see each other for 26 years, and my friend does not write, we kept up with each others lives through periodic phone calls salted with love.

My girlfriend welcomed my visit for her big 60th birthday bash, and while others were amazed that we had kept up all those years without seeing each other in person, we girlfriends continued with our girl talk as if it had been yesterday when we last saw each other.

This sweet friend had recently experienced the joys of becoming a first-time grandma and couldn't wait to spread the delight of this uniquely special occasion by sending me a most thoughtful first-time grandma gift: a little rocking chair with our grandson's name painted on the back ~ ah, so very adorable.

I created a card for my friend and wrote:"There is a magic to our long-distance friendship ~ a grace and power that defies explanation (to others)."

Julie to Jules

On the occasion of thanking you for my sweet remembrance as I am a first time grandma

Caleb's rocking chair is perfect. Thank you, Jules!

When I was visiting my friend last year, Jules' kindhearted son, Matt, took the day off from work to drive us around. When Matt drove us to Jones Beach, this commemorative corner caused me to pause and take a photograph. This is one of many memorials in New York to honor the victims, the heroes, and the volunteers of 9/11 ~ today it is hard for me not to think of all the grandparents and grandchildren who will never get the opportunity to know one another...

**Perfect love sometimes does not come
Until the first grandchild.**
Welsh Proverb

**When a child is born,
So are grandmothers.**
Judith Levy

Amy

Why My Daddy is Bald

This is the story of an eight-year-old boy who was teased and bullied at school and in the play ground of the day care center because his Daddy was bald.

Robert was looking through the fence of the day care center, watching for his Dad's green truck to come up the driveway to get him.

Every day after school, he and number of other children from his school would ride the bus to the day care center where they would stay until their parents came for them after they got out of work.

He was most anxious this day as some boys at school and the bigger boys at the day care center had been extra mean to him that day, calling him names and saying bad things about his Dad because he was bald.

Finally, his Dad was there... He ran to the truck, jumped in, and gave his Dad's leg a big hug. "Hi buddy, how ya' doing," says his Dad as they pulled into the traffic. There was a long silence. "Some of your friends were watching you when I pulled up the driveway," he continued.

"They're not my friends, Dad, and, I don't like being around them or with them."

"There is something going on at school or in the play ground that is really bothering you, maybe more so today than other days, that's right, isn't it?" asks Dad.

"Yes, but I can't tell you about it, Dad."

"If you talk about, it will something bad happen...do you think?" asked Dad. Tears began to well up in Robert's eyes.

"Dad, will you please let your hair grow back on your head, and then...   I won't have to worry that something bad will happen to you, and those boys will be my friends and be nice to me?"

"Oh, Robert, you are being hurt, and you think my safety is being threatened. I am so sorry this is happening to you. First of all, bullies and threats will not be tolerated for any reason, and secondly, these boys need to be educated on why many people are bald.

Robert, do you remember when we went on a summer vacation to Aunt Stephanie's cabin in the mountains of Colorado?"

"Yes, Dad I do...Aunt Stephie was very sick."

"That's right... A few months before that, she had breast cancer and had an operation called a mastectomy. Afterward, Grandma stayed at her house to take care of her. When her body had healed, she started a treatment called chemotherapy to make sure all of the cancer cells in her body would be killed. There are many side effects to these treatments which last several months. One thing that happens is that you lose all of the hair on your body."

"Robert, if something happened to your sister, would you want to show her that you loved her and supported her in any way that you could?"

"Oh yes, Dad... I love De De, and I would do anything to help her."

"I love my sister, too, very much, and I wanted to show her that I loved her and would do anything to help her get well and to support her."

"One morning, when I was praying for her and looking in the mirror, I thought, I could shave my head. If she was going to be bald, I could be bald, too. So I did. I shaved my head."

"When I went into work that morning, I was teased, called names, and people asked me if I thought I was trying to be some big, movie star, and then said that I wasn't going to cut it in that role.

When the break room was full, I stood up and told this group: My sister, whom I love dearly, has breast cancer. Besides being very sick, she is going through chemo and has lost all of her hair. That can be an awful thing for a woman to go through. I decided to show my support for my sister and become bald too... I wasn't trying to be macho or act like a movie star... I just wanted to let my sister know that I love her and that she is always in my thoughts and prayers."

"There was silence in the room. Then, guys came up to me and said they were sorry for their comments, and they hoped my sister would be OK. Do you know, to this day, people come up to me and ask how my sister is doing."

"All that day when I was out on my route, I told people why I was bald...Everyone respected me. When I got home that evening, your Mommy told me she thought I was pretty handsome, and that even after Aunt Stephie got her hair back maybe I should stay bald."

"Then she told me she had signed up for the Cow Town Marathon which supported Breast Cancer Research. Your Mommy ran that race along with a thousand other people."

"When we were with Aunt Stephie in Colorado, she had just a few hairs on her head... I told her I shaved my head every morning, and I could shave hers, too, and get rid of all the straggly hairs she had left on her head. So, we went to the bathroom, and I did it.

Later that week, she was feeling a little better, and she took you and me to a ghost town. She had a scarf on her head and we took pictures. You took a picture of her and me in the window of an empty old gold miner's cabin."

"It is grandma's favorite picture of her son, your daddy, and her daughter, your Aunt Stephie. We also had a neighbor take a family picture of all of us. Aunt Stephie and I are bald."

"Several months later, Aunt Stephie was feeling much better and her hair started growing back on her head. She even adopted three sheltie dogs from Sheltie Rescue."

"Today, Aunt Stephie is totally well, and, I am STILL bald, to honor and support all people who had cancer."

"Now, I think, we need to tell this story at your school. I am sure there are lots of children who know someone who has had breast cancer and other cancers, even little children have cancer...Due to their treatment of this disease, they have lost their hair or have other deformities. There is no reason to tease or bully these people or any of their family members. They need our love, our support, our compassion, our understanding, and most of all, our prayers."

"I agree Dad, let's tell this story at my school."

Julie

**May God keep you from all harm.
May God guide and bless you more and more.
May today be even a better day,
Than the day you had before.**

**Lavender lives here
No plumbs for munching
Nor wine to sip in the sun
Thankful for purple**

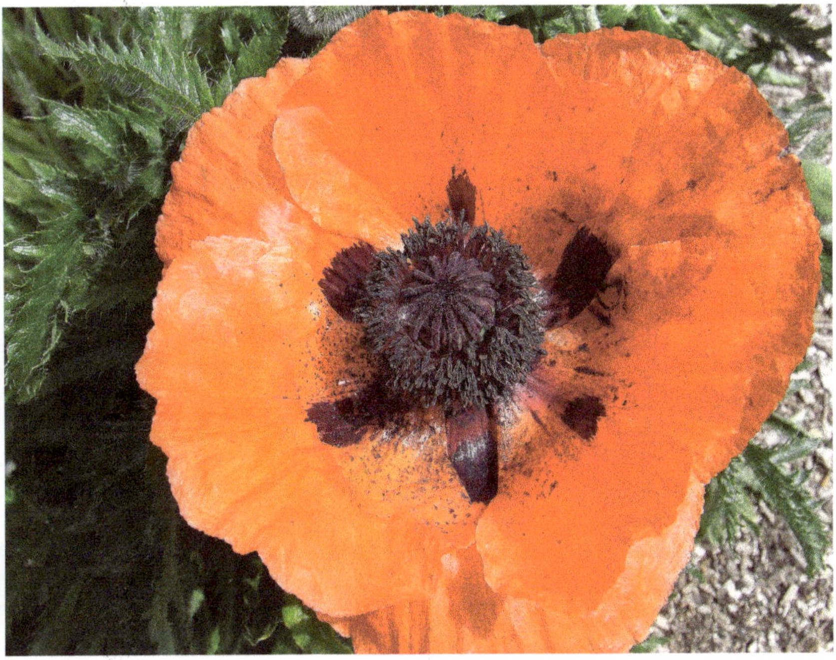

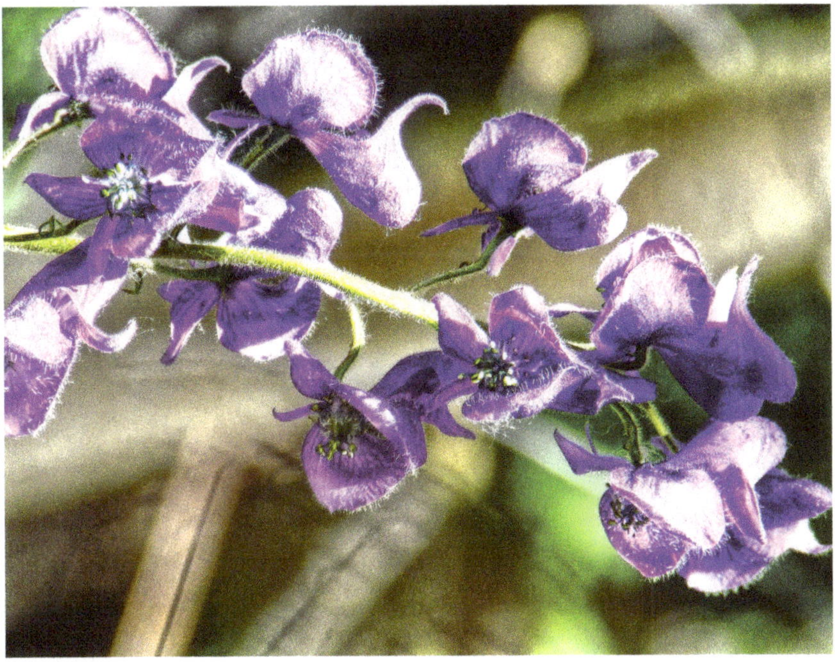

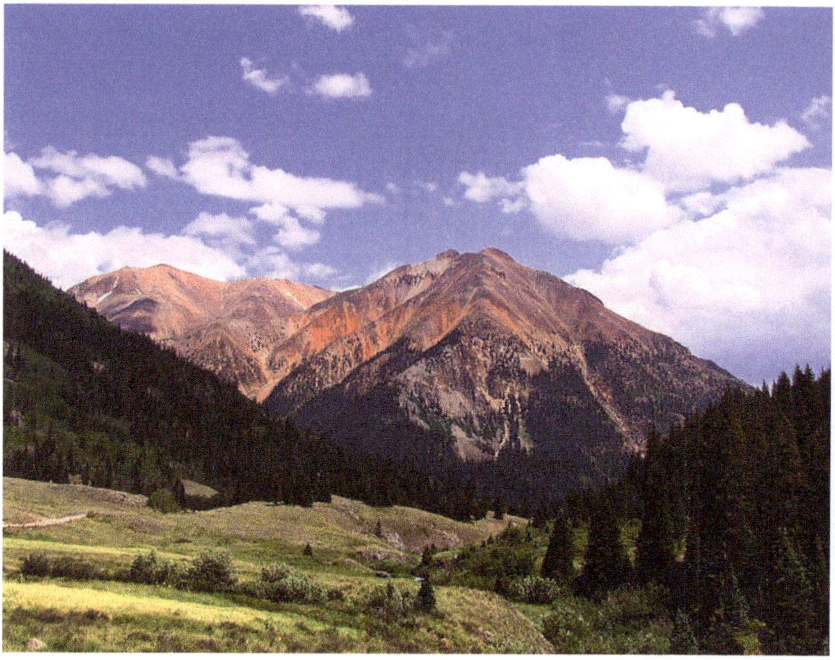

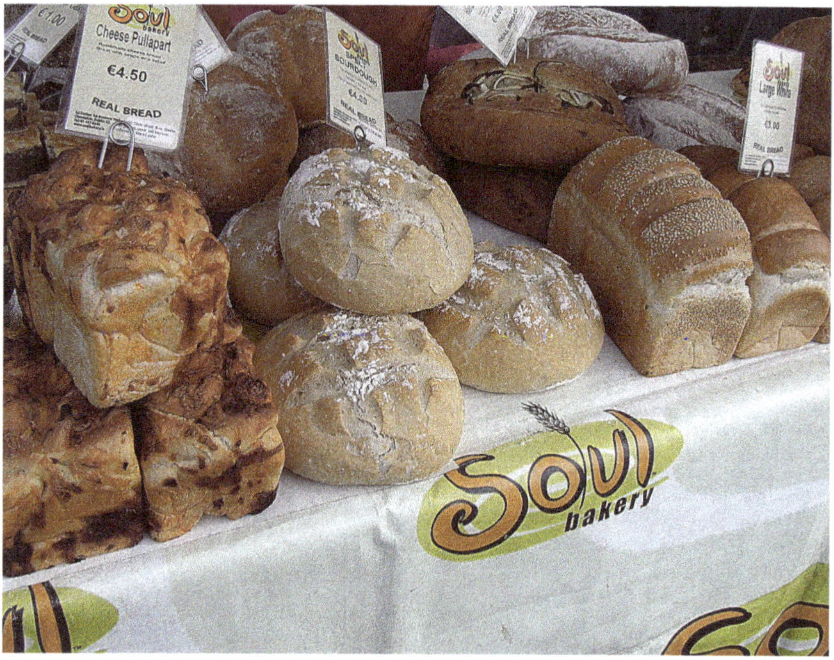

**You cannot be at the top of the mountain
and at the bottom of the ocean
At the same time
You must make a decision
Choose your colors**

This is one of my favorite pictures from Howth, Ireland, a side trip when my husband and I visited our son and his wife, when they were living in Dublin, Ireland in the autumn of 2009. We had some of our amazing Ireland adventures on side trips. One was to Howth where they were having a farmer's market. This beautiful, delicious looking bread begged to be photographed. Bread is the staff of life.

Two of my favorite poets wrote:

**I am going to learn to make bread tomorrow.
So you may imagine me with my sleeves
rolled up, mixing flour, milk, saleratus, etc.,
with a deal of grace.
I advise you if you don't know how to make
the staff of life to learn with dispatch.**
Emily Dickinson

**If thou tastest a crust of bread,
Thou tastest all the stars
And all the heavens.**
Robert Browning

**Bread is the warmest, kindest of all words.
Write it always with a capital letter,
like your own name.**
from a café sign

**Bread - So you never go hungry.
Wine - So your life is always sweet.
Salt - So there is always spice in your life.**
from "It's a Wonderful Life"
One of my favorite movies

**A Jug of Wine,
a Loaf of Bread
and Thou**
The Rubáiyát of Omar Khayyám
One of my favorite poems

One of my favorite prayers, the traditional version I grew up with:

> **Our Father, Who art in heaven**
> **Hallowed be Thy Name;**
> **Thy kingdom come,**
> **Thy will be done,**
> **On earth as it is in heaven.**
> **Give us this day our daily bread,**
> **And forgive us our trespasses,**
> **As we forgive those who trespass against us**
> **And lead us not into temptation,**
> **But deliver us from evil.**
> **Amen.**

Though I like using the word "sins" instead of trespasses – let us not pretty it up.

When I was growing up, we recited this grace before meals:

> **Bless us, Oh Lord,**
> **And these thy gifts which**
> **We are about to receive from thy bounty,**
> **Through Christ, Our Lord.**
> **Amen.**

I say 'recite' rather than 'prayed', because when a prayer is repeated so many times that you don't have to think about it, but rather begin to reel it off by memory, well, that becomes reciting rather than praying. One day my mother simply said from now on we are going to make up our own prayer before meals, and everyone took their turn. While she was usually completely wrapped up in all the church bric-a-brac, this was definitely one of her finer moments.

We might have prayed:

> Thank you God
> For this beautiful day
> And for the delicious,
> Hot, homemade bread
> And the tomatoes from our garden,
> And thank you for us all
> Being here to enjoy it together,
> And bless the hands
> That prepared this food.
> Amen

Amy

Sammy was a stray dog that lived on the peninsula where our family came every weekend to build our house. It was 1986. A shepherd/lab mix, he was big and strong,"King of the Point." The weekenders gave him scraps, but we gave him the premium food our dogs ate.

The years had taken their toll on him. By 2002, he no longer was "The King." He knew when we were at the lake house, hanging around when we were there. All of a sudden, he was gone. I looked all over for him. My neighbor told me the last time she saw him was on July 4th running down the street when all the fire crackers started. He hated loud noises. I surmised he had been scared to death. One morning, when I was sitting on the dock, I could feel his presence and wrote, "The Smile of Sammy."

The Smile of Sammy

**Where have you gone, I know not where I
looked for you here and there
Whenever you saw me, you'd speed your trot
Almost came running as you always got
A special touch of my Love as I would pet you
Each time I greeted you, Sammy so dear
I always thanked God you were still here.**

**As I sit on this dock today and remember you I
can almost feel the roughness of your paw
As you would beg for me to love you more You
know Sammy, when I fed you
It also fed my soul.**

At the end of my stay,
As I'd get ready to leave
I would always pray for you and believed God
blessed you, loved you, protected you
This Homeless Wondering One

Oh, Sammy, Where have you gone
I know not where
To Heaven to rump and run
Where thunderstorms will
Never scare anyone.
Rest in peace my special Friend
I love you and will miss you
The Smile of you Sammy, so Dear

Big Date at Bass Lake
(written June 2005)

I have a big Date
My visit at Bass Lake

Looking so forward to Great Fellowship,
Delicious food, laughter

Maybe a few tears
Prayers Relevant and Dear
To hear the Apostles Creed
Brought past memories Indeed

And then there is the JOKE
Serviettes, never to be wasted or smeared!

Helen and I just seem to connect,
Thinking a like
As water running through a hole in a dike The sister perhaps that I never had. Listening to Bob and Dean Chatting away
Computers, Automobiles,

Chopping the tree
Warmed my heart to see

My special desire: morning, noon and night
A dip in Bass Lake – Oh, so Cold
One has to be bold
Refreshment prevails and coldness derails
A thrilling experience for Body and Soul

Now the end has come to our stay
I'll try not to be sad, as we drive away
Remembering the graciousness of Helen
The wit of Dear Dean
Strength of Both, Faith so Strong

And Little Brave heart meowing a song
Sunrise, sunsets, magnificent skies
Splashes of the Lake as water makes a wake
Feeling the cool breeze – Hearing the loons

As the awe of nature abounds
Thank you, dear Lord,
For sounds and sights
For these are the creations
Of your Powerful Might

My brother-in-law is big on genealogy, doing both sides of his parents' families. From this has come Family Reunions, the first one of which was held in Ottawa, Canada since the majority of the Purdy's live there. I had briefly met Helen and the Rev. Dean Purdy years ago. I told my husband if we were going, a 1500 mile trip, that I wanted to stay at Bass Lake where Helen and Dean live. The Reunion was awesome for me, this person who never had an extended family. I wrote My Big Date at Bass Lake while sitting on the long stairway leading down to Bass Lake.

Bass Lake in the Tub

**This morning I took a hot bath
To let the travel muscles relax.
When at the end
The spigot I did bend
Far to the right – cold water to make
So I could pretend I was once again
In refreshing Bass Lake.**

This was written the day after we camehome from the Purdy reunion and our stay at Bass Lake.

Julie

An Idea is Born
**Suddenly
As pink catches my eye
An idea is born,
Unfolding
As full-blown rose.**

As a flash of pink caught my eye, this wild rose was found on a morning hike around Gold Hill, sprinkled softly with droplets of rain from a storm the previous night.

A hike is a little miracle – getting the body to work correctly all at the same time, while processing thoughts about what we see and how we are touched emotionally by the nest of robin's eggs, raindrops on rose petals or clouds stroking the mountaintops like snow, - whatever our problems, if we ignore our blessings, our problems are bigger than we ever perceived.

We are all in the same leaky boat, but as long as we feel another's hand in ours, see the brilliant contrast of red geranium in the blue thrift store flowerpot, hear our puppy whine for her morning walk, get a brain freeze from a frozen treat, take that picture at the precise moment the bird is approaching lift-off, create a poem that fits just right with the photograph...really see American Basin...really see the morning sunshine creating shapes and shadows through our own kitchen window...really see the filtered sunlight through the tree in our own back- yard...we are alive for now...right now...this moment is all we really have. Do we see that?

I like the mornings best. It is a clean slate. I like at the close of our day when my husband asks if I had a good day, hoping the answer is yes. A very good day. Someone cares.

I help a student create a haiku or a drawing she is proud of. I construct just the right card for a friend, or I say just the right comforting word at the moment it is needed. For that moment I have made a difference. That moment is all that matters for awhile. Life is a matter of moments.

It is now 'ordinary time' in the church for Catholic and Episcopal and other denominations that follow this custom. I like the way that sounds ~ ordinary time ~ I see laundry stirring in the breeze on the clothes line, grandmother and grandchild baking cookies together, enjoying cutting out different shapes in the dough, lovers holding hands, a new dad soothing his baby son, the smell of freshly cut grass, a puppy barking in wonderment at a leaf blowing across the yard, a friend telephoning or writing another...

The best thing in church yesterday was Lisa coming up behind me and throwing her arms around my neck, thanking me for the rose card that I made for her.

**Some people never say the words
'I love you'.
It's not their style to be so bold.
Some people never say those words:
'I love you'
But, like a child,
They're longing to be told.**
Paul Simon

44

How do you like to go up in a swing,
Up in the air so blue?
Oh, I do think it the pleasantest thing
Ever a child can do!

Up in the air and over the wall,
Till I can see so wide,
River and trees and cattle and all
Over the countryside—

Till I look down on the garden green,
Down on the roof so brown—
Up in the air I go flying again,
Up in the air and down!

Robert Louis Stevenson

This cooling moment when the red sun Relaxes
to bathe the mountainside pink,
Earth is softened
Nature is mellowed, delicate,
Yielding to the chilly rosy sky
Simply seen as though through a child's eye
This holy light of night.

October is "Breast Cancer Awareness Month" when pink is highlighted. The pink sunset of Crystal Peak is a reminder of Stephanie's story and the continued search for a cure.

Amy

MacTavish's Tender Kiss

    This poem is about my 17 month old grandson, Robert, who for the first time, stayed overnight with us. When he woke up in the middle of the night crying, I brought him to our room and sitting on the edge of the bed, gently rocked him. MacTavish, our Sheltie, is fearful of small children, having been injured by a child when he was a puppy. He keeps his distance from Robert. As he continued to cry, MacTavish jumped up on the end of the bed and was slowing creeping closer to us. When he was next to us, he licked Robert's little feet. The crying becomes a whimper. Robert giggled and petted the dog. MacTavish then gave Robert a big lick on his cheek. Robert was content and slept the rest of the night in his crib. The next day, I wrote "The Happy Face" it was February 2002.

The Happy Face

**I sit here in this now quiet room Looking
at all the toys a strewn
I see a little happy face
That bounces all over the place.
And MacTavish, you were so very dear
Telling Robert in the middle of the night
Do not fear
Back to sleep you went
With the love of God sent**

Guilt produced this poem...so many birthday cards never written or mailed on time. Mother's Day was upon me and I decided to make amends by sending this to all my women friends.

Happy Mother's Day

Recently, I lost (misplaced) a small card holder.
Inside the house,
At least I'd hoped it was here
Not lost out in the World somewhere

The one credit card had no activity
When I canceled it. This little purse
Did have money that I had stashed
As I never ever wanted to be broke.

The house was turned upside down Straightened out my underwear drawer Cleaned out the closet, now that was a scare
Even my desk was not to be spared.
Looking under, over, inside behind,
The little purse was nowhere to be found

In the midst of the search, I found
Old birthday cards, letters and notes
From friends, co-workers, my beautiful daughter, even my mother.

Things of the past   that I had saved
And could not put down.
The thought then struck I will never be broke For my friends are Wonderful and True.

For the past year or so,
I have not been good at sending birthday cards
Or thank you notes when they were due.
To remember and let you know,

You're in my thoughts and Prayers too
I send you Love and Joy for a special Happy
Mother's Day
May all your Wishes come true.

Something unexpected had come up, and I needed to leave the house. Bob was out fishing. I was sure he was close to the point at the end of our road, and if I rode my bike down there, I could get his attention, and let him know that I would be gone when he returned home. He was so engrossed in catching the big one, he never did see me... I rode back home and wrote this poem for him. A love note...

The Bike Ride

Never realized before,
We live on a little Hill
The coast down was an easy Bill

The seat is a little high
My poor butt, Oh My

I saw you out there fishing
But you were missing

The sight of my moves
As my boobs were bouncing by

See you tonight
Love ya lots.

Big T's

On the evening of February 13th, I had put the finishing touches on a Valentine poem I had written for my co-workers for the kindness they had shown to me. The hour was quite late, but I had one more important card to write. This one was to my wonderful husband of forty plus years whose wood carving talent and creativity had recently unfolded for the joy of both of us and our terrific children, Stephanie, Bobby and Angela... Poetry allows me to let people know how truly special they are, sometimes provides a laugh, but always a smile.

**Happy Valentine's Day
Dear Bob**

**To the Love of my Life
Your creativity is vivid and Bold
No wonder I have been Sold
And for all these Years Untold
My pen is now Pooped
I sit here in a Swoop
I'll say Good Night
For tomorrow we'll fly our Kites
With dreams and Schemes
For our Delights**

I found this half-finished poem when I was looking for something else; it was Christmas and my husband was out playing golf that day, so I finished it up. I'd not written anything for a long time and it felt good.

To Play or Not Too Play

Twas the day before Christmas
And the sun arose in a warm blaze...
My golf clubs sat in the corner
Gathering dust in a daze...

Should I call my buddies?
To play a quick round or
Must I be good and leave
My creative mind in a mound

When all of a sudden
The cell phone did ring
And I was forced to answer the darn thing
Lo and behold it was
Bobby Lee wanting to play

While mama was on her
Last minute shopping spree
We jumped in the car
And sped to the course
A little excited and full of glee

The place was closed...OH MY...
We snuck in behind the big tree
A hole or two played,
A few sips of the sauce
Ah...we felt much like a big boss

Back home again with a feeling of pride Twas the day before Christmas
These two ole men, like two little boys Were just kind of tickled inside
Wondering what else Santa could hide

Julie

Though it was a crowded, July day at the peak of perfection, I did not see the other people who were there, nor did I feel the clouds of mosquitoes that the generous rainfall brought along with the glorious wildflowers.

American Basin offers one of the most spectacular basin views in the San Juan Mountains. It is especially impressive in late July and early August when the wildflowers weave a colorful quilt. Picturesque Sloan Lake can be reached by way of the American Basin Trail. Hiking can continue up to Handies Peak, one of five 14,000 foot peaks in the area. From personal experience I can say that the view from the top of Handies Peak is one of the best in the San Juan Mountains. The peak, at 14,048 feet, offers a panoramic view of the San Juan Mountains. Please be careful to stay on the trail to avoid erosion on the fragile tundra.

Typically, July and August afternoons bring thunder showers up in the mountains. Avoid the peak, ridges, and open areas during a storm. It is best to get an early start. Hiking at high altitude requires more time and energy. To be safe, make sure some- one knows where you are going and when you plan to return. Not picking one blossom is true on the tundra where I have heard that blooms can take up to two hundred years to grow...

**Earth laughs
In flowers.**
Ralph Waldo Emerson, "Hamatreya"

I will be the gladdest thing under the sun! I will touch a hundred flowers and not pick one.
Edna St. Vincent Millay, "Afternoon on a Hill"

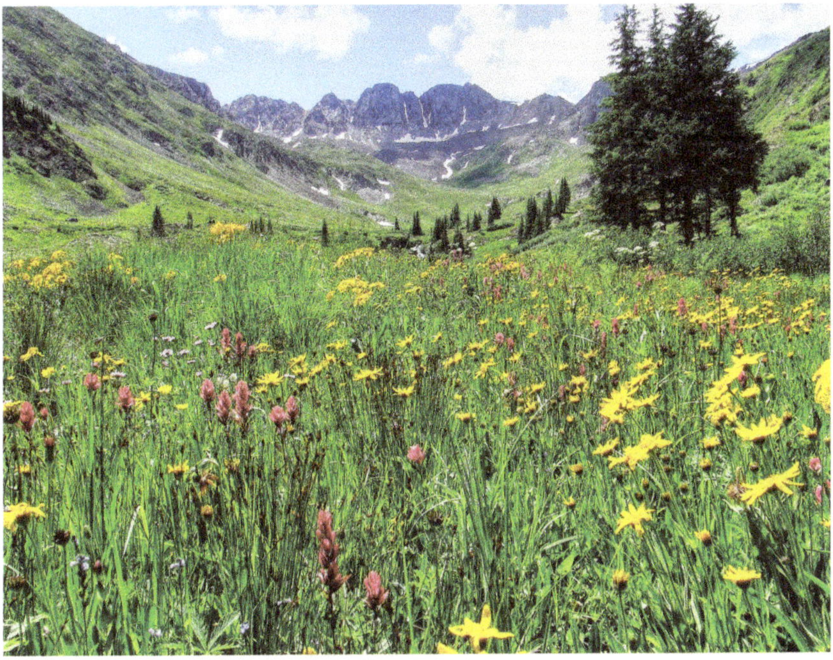

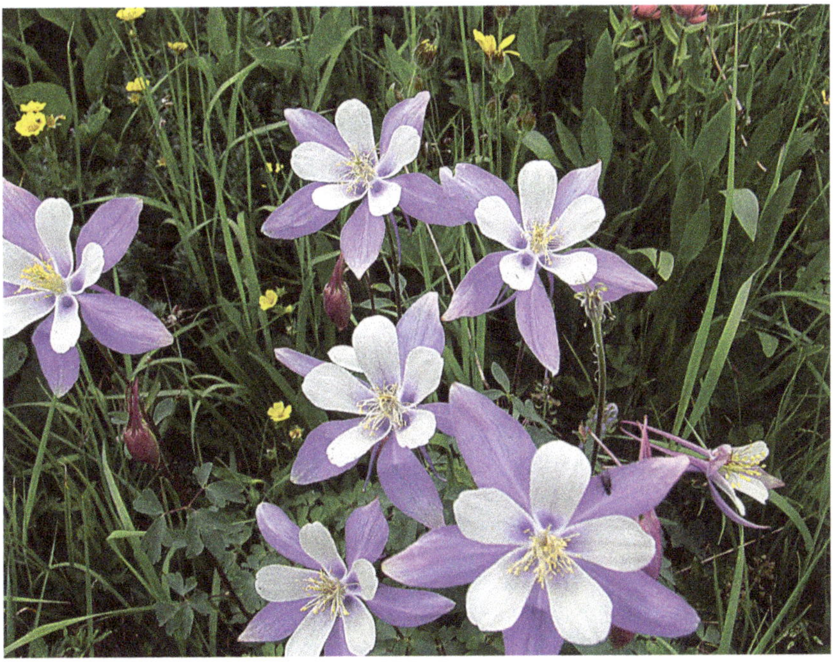

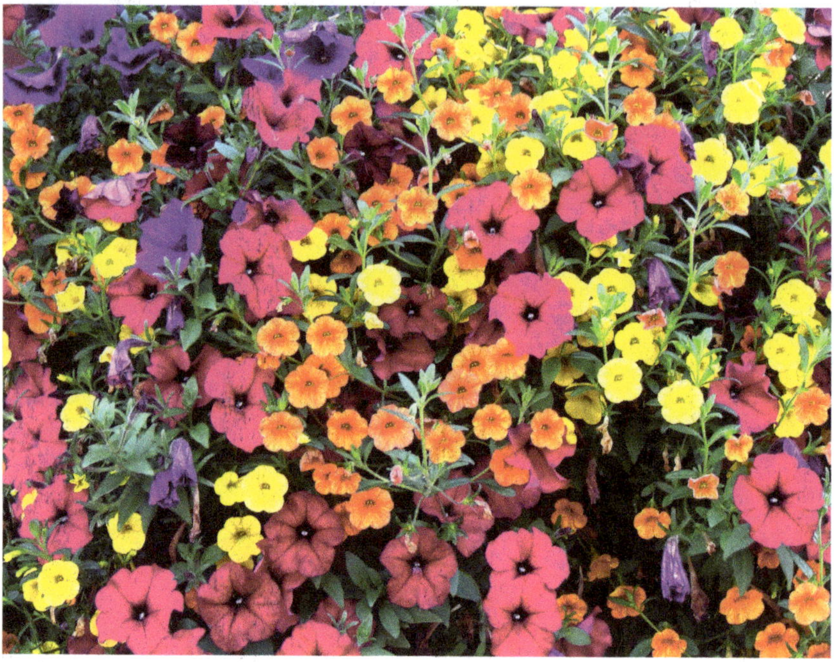

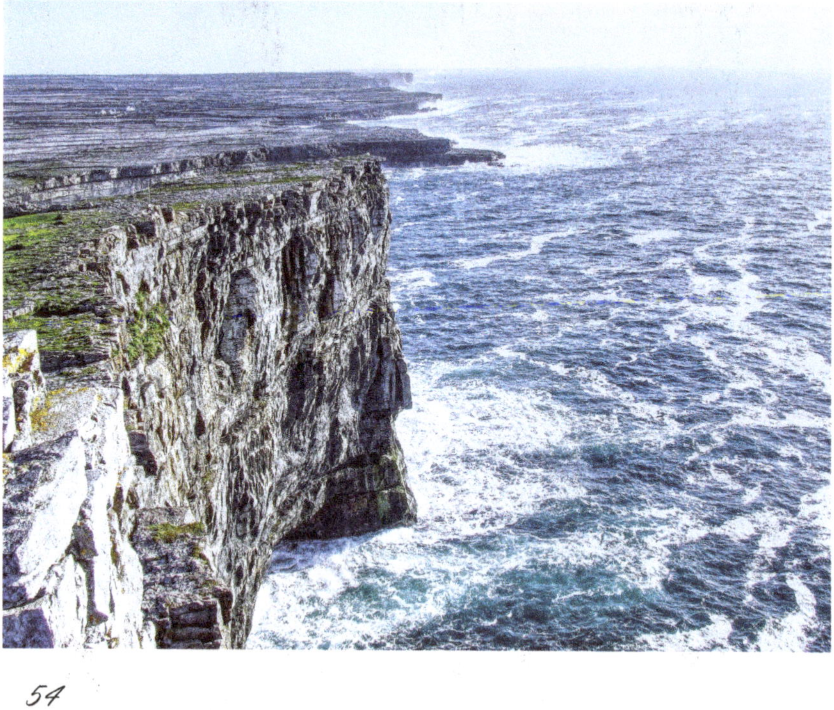

This colorful picture just makes me happy ~ in part because it was taken on an Amy and Julie adventure, and because I love the joy flowers give, freely.

Keep love blooming ~ celebrate special days.

Flowers
God finger-painting

There is a pleasure in the pathless woods,
There is a rapture on the lonely shore,
There is society, where none intrudes, By
the deep sea, and music in its roar: I love
not man the less, but Nature more.
George Gordon,
Lord Byron, Childe Harold's Pilgrimage

Why do we love the sea?
It is because it has some potent power To
make us think things we like to think.
Robert Henri

I was born loving the beach...the smell and sound of the pounding surf...the feel of the cool sand between my toes...long walks on the shore...the cries of the seagulls...the sun on my body...discovering treasures of seashells...early strolls in the coolness of the morning...fireball sunsets on the horizon...the glittering, effervescent light in the seawater at night.

My ability to draw peaked in the third grade, and it was not too good even then, therefore, to me, what some people can create out of barrenness is nothing short of prodigious.

When I was a little girl living in Metairie, Louisiana, Pontchartrain Beach was where we spent some of our free days. Since childhood, I have experienced 'the beach' in the different settings of lakes and oceans.

A Day at the Beach

A castle of sand
Picnic surrounded by surf
Effervescent waves

Does he paint?
He fain would write a poem, does he write?
He fain would paint a picture.
Robert Browning

My brilliant daughter does both! So much love went into this painting. A bit of our soul goes into the art we create. She and I talked about going to Mexico to see the butterflies for my 50th birthday. The trip has not happened...yet; but her beautiful painting of the monarchs did.

Amy

The holidays always lend themselves for creative expression. Since I usually want to do something different for our personal greeting cards, I would write a poem or story, and Bob would choose a photograph from our year to compliment my work. These are a few of my favorite Christmas messages.

Christmas 2005

**As we do grow older
Share, our joys, our sorrows,
Our laughs and our tears
We give thanks for
Our precious Family
And our Friendship with you**

**Busy Busy
Excitement Reigns
Exhaustion too
From little Children to Grumpy Old Men -
And a few women too**

**We stop in Silence and Wonder
As we remember**

**Celebrate the Joy of Life
For it all began with
The Birth and Love of Christ**

Christmas 2008

**Mercy   Grace   Forgiveness   Love Precious
Gifts from our Lord
Receive and Accept**

**Disperse and Give them away
To the World this Holiday Season
Sending you these Gifts with Much Love**

The "season" brings out so many different emotions in all of us… from creativeness and fun, to stress and depression. When I wrote this poem, it occurred to me that it didn't bring out the real reason for Christmas… Christ Jesus. As you eat this chocolate, be mindful of God's love for you, and the love and thankfulness Bob and I have for you, our friends and precious family.

The Chocolate Bar

**It was two (2) weeks before December 25th Our
Workshops were piled High
Are you sure this is Christmas
We said with a Sigh!**

**Amy's in her sewing room
Bob in his Wood Shop
Projects were starting to POP**

**All activity was going like a Blaze
The Sawdust in the air
Was Making a Haze**

As progress is booming
Our Hearts are kept Light
I just hope we can finish
By Christmas Eve Night.

We wanted you to know
How important you Are
So instead of a drink
We bought you the this Chocolate Bar

This treat comes with Holiday Cheer Cause
it smells a lot better
Than tiny Reindeer

Morning Prayer
(Written December 2005)

Our Heavenly Father
Guide Me through this Day
You know I have so Many things
I want to accomplish today

Help me, Lord, to Remember,
That it is in Your Will and Your Day
So I can do these chores, Your Way

When frustration Hits,
And my back aches, and feels like it will
crack into tiny bits
It is time for me to take a break, and Rest

Lord, you're telling me that would be Best
Guide me Lord, through this Day
Reminding me to do it Your Way.

I was hurting pretty bad when I wrote this and had too many things I wanted to get done. Early morning, sitting on the dock overlooking the lake is a good time for reflection and meditation.

Sleepless Night

Why Can't I Sleep
I bounce around from head to toe
Wondering when the Sandman might show
Then, my tummy starts to say
Gee, I'm hungry can't you see
Milk and Cookies sure would satisfy me.

How many times do we toss and turn and hope that sleep might come soon? One night, I just got up and had cookies and milk, then went back to bed and slept.

Bob and Amy's Place

Bob was delighted
That Amy got sighted
(She retired from American Airlines)

To their Winnsboro lake House
They have moved
The Octagon Place
That has lots of space

Where the Sun rises over the trees,
The fresh smell of a gentle cool breeze
Washes ripples of water
Up to the lake shore

Listen----you hear all of nature's lore
The Woodpecker is making another hole

To "Dock Sit" this way
At the start of each new day
Is God's Wonderful Blessing Behold

Lots of work has began
Unpacking STILL not done
Build, paint, fix, clean out the old
A little golfing, a little fishing
And lots of digging

Read, Write and Create
More "To Dos" for her Mate
They are generously told
For Amy's imagination does unfold!

No matter what stresses
Or messes have come up like a mole
Calm and Serenity
Still envelopes the Soul.

Julie

In Ireland, our family went bicycling on the largest Aran Island, Inishmore. At daybreak we came upon a huge, Celtic cross being bathed in the warm sunrise. The moment was like a prayer of thanksgiving for such a glorious morning after a cold, rainy night. The locals said that picturesque days, like we were blessed with, are a rare exception.

One of many popular legends about St. Patrick in Ireland links the saint with the Celtic cross. It has been said that Patrick combined the symbol of Christianity with the sun cross, to give pagan followers an idea of the importance of the cross, by linking it with the idea of the life-giving properties of the sun.

> **Everybody needs beauty**
> **As well as bread,**
> **Places to play in and pray in,**
> **Where nature may heal**
> **And give strength to body and soul.**
> John Muir

> **I thank you God for this most amazing day,**
> **For the leaping greenly spirits of trees,**
> **And for the blue dream of sky**
> **And for everything which is natural,**
> **Which is infinite,**
> **Which is yes.**
> E.E. Cummings

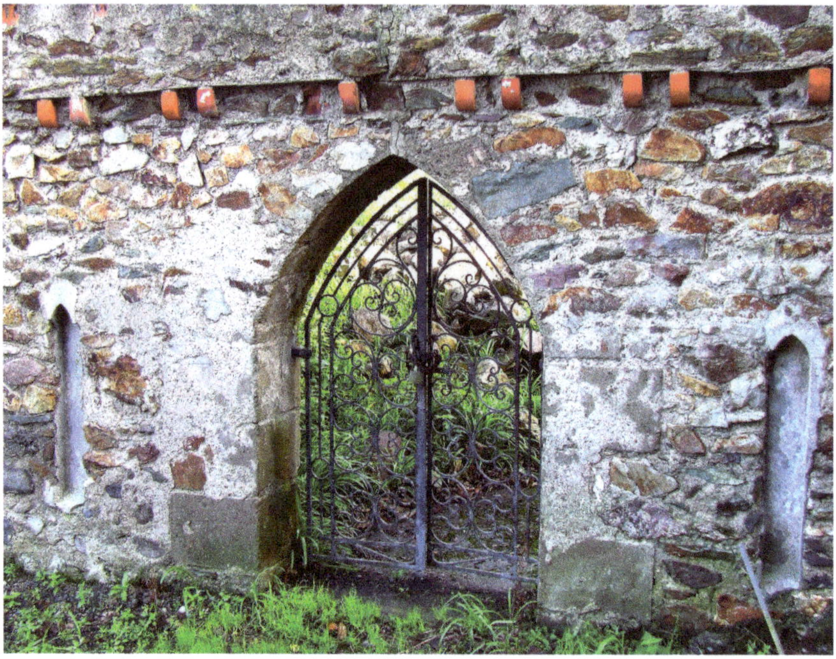

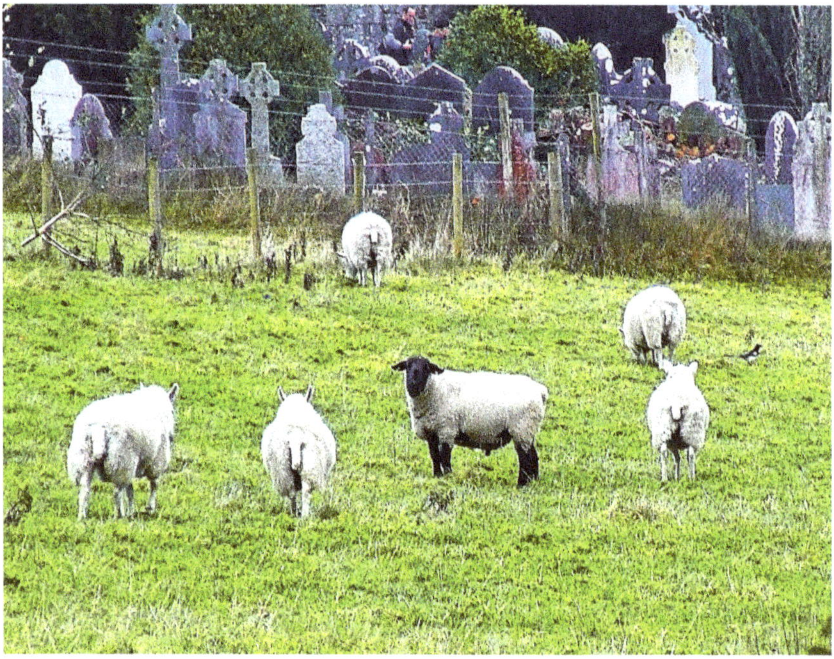

Howth, originally a small fishing village, is now a suburb of Dublin, Ireland. This unexpected gate called out to be photographed. Stories are always running through my mind. As in other tales depicting the wardrobe or the rabbit hole, there is a story waiting to unfold on the other side...

**We cannot possibly know
What is on the other side
Unless we do go
Through the gate.**

Enter the gates with Thanksgiving
Psalm 100

**The world is all gates, all opportunities,
strings of tension waiting to be struck.**
Ralph Waldo Emerson

**Love is the master key
Which opens the gates of happiness.**
Oliver Wendell Holmes

It is good to travel and to have experiences outside of our comfort corner. Like lost sheep, we sometimes wander around looking for greener pasture, hoping we find it before we run out of time. It seems there is often a burial ground nearby to remind us that there is never enough time...

**Travel is fatal to prejudice, bigotry,
and narrow-mindedness.**
Mark Twain

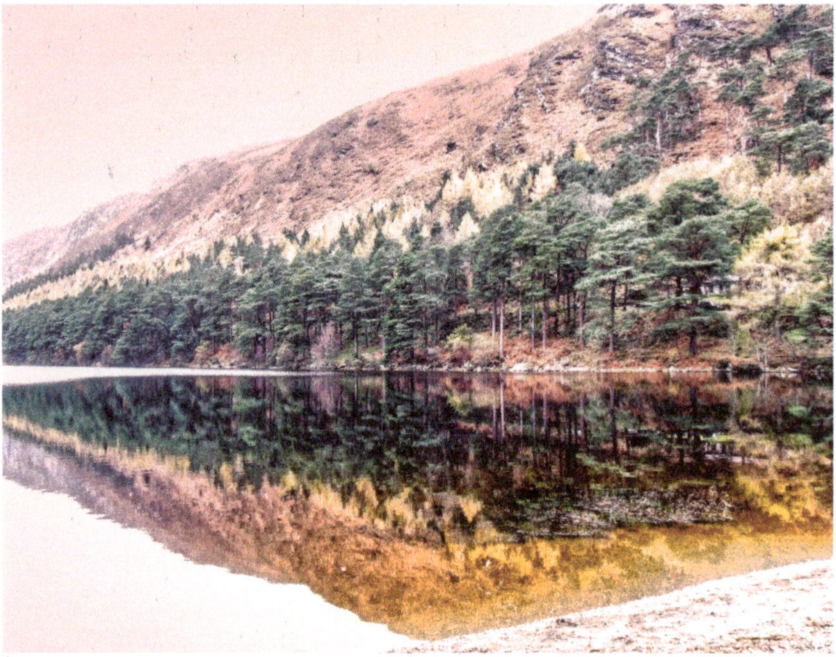

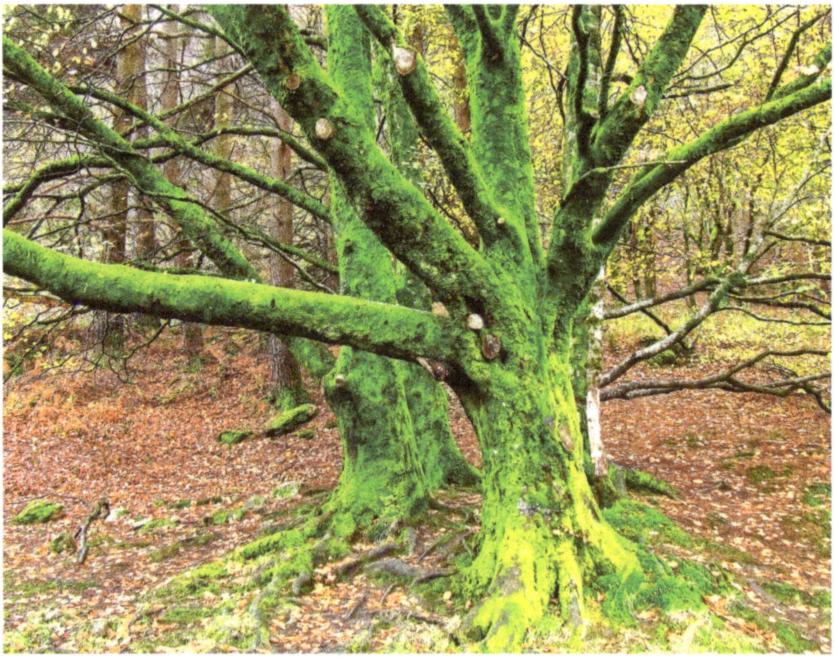

Glendalough, meaning glen of two lakes, is a glacial valley located in County Wicklow, Ireland. I took this photograph of a lake reflecting the November colors. The scene carries me into a nook of emotion. Glendalough is like walking through a fairytale. Enchantment overtook the senses. In the forest I saw gnomes sitting beneath giant, red and white polka dotted mushrooms, there were unicorns, and fairies dancing under waterfalls.

Reflection

**Like Alice's glass
I see something not quite there
Reflections in me**

Not perhaps Kilmer's tree, yet a stunning illustration of poetry in the form of a tree.

Blessed be the tree. Trees, like people, worship with zeal in the wind and with tranquility in the sunshine, but trees, unlike people, never spoil their surroundings.

Silky Emerald Tree

**Silky emerald
Unicorn or fairy dance
Enchantment in thee**

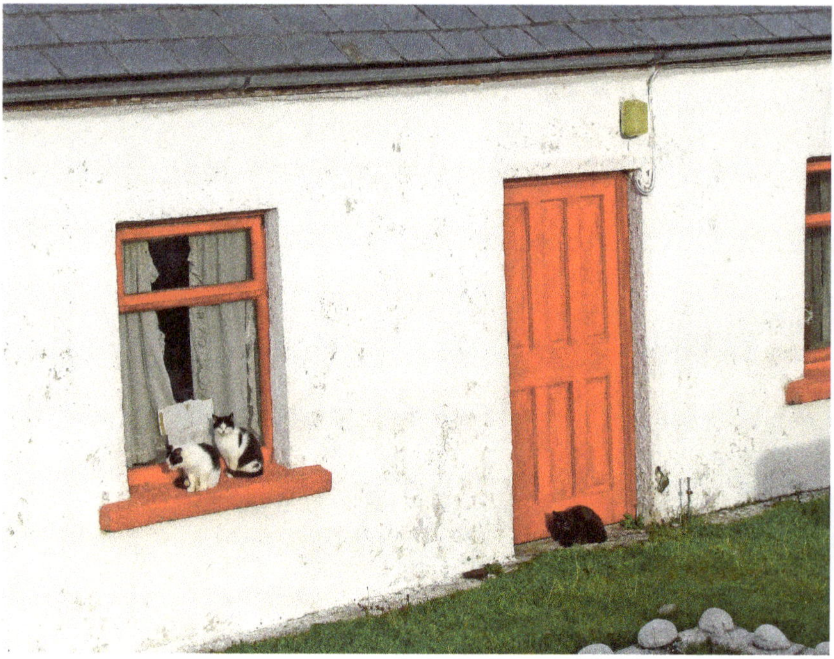

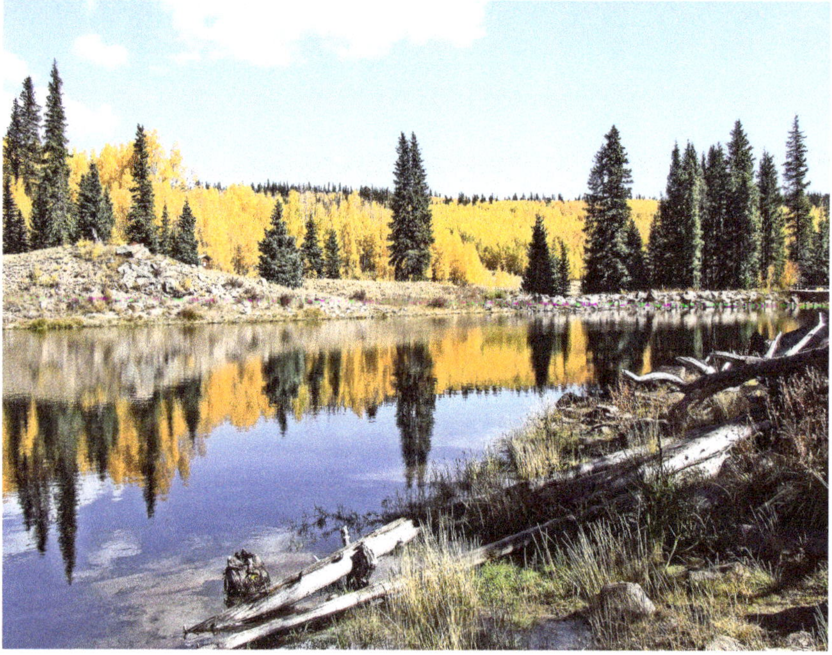

Our Cottage

**A cottage dwelling
Domestic tranquility
My family's abode**

    A Gaelic treat, this cottage photograph was taken as we bicycled on Inishmore, Aran Islands, Ireland.
    For me a cottage evokes an ordinary time of washing socks, chopping onion, quarreling and kissing, feeding the cat and walking the dog, star gazing, and reading by the fire.

I can envision a small cottage somewhere, with a lot of writing paper, and a dog, and a fireplace and maybe enough money to give myself some Irish coffee now and then and to entertain my two friends.
Lt. Richard Van de Geer

*I've always regarded nature
as the clothing of God.*
Alan Hovhaness

The Lake in Autumn

**Golden on sapphire
Silence becomes breathtaking
Honey glides downhill.**

Angela's Quilt

Our son's first marriage of one year ended in divorce. Bobby was 28, and it was several years before he started to think about dating. While he was on one of his sales routes, the manager of that store asked him if he had noticed Angela, the girl in the office. He noticed, but was apprehensive about beginning a relationship. Angela,   while separated for two years, was not yet divorced, and was also cautious about whom she would let into her life. Eventually, they began seeing one another.
More than anything, Bobby wanted a wife and a family. We gave him credit for all of his efforts with Angela's children. The road was bumpy, and he knew that he had many challenges ahead. He was the strong, caring, male role model that Kyle, 13, and Melissa, 12, needed.
A year or so after her divorce, they discussed getting married. At first they did not want Bob and I present at the ceremony. Bob told Bobby that we 'wanted to be a part of his family, and we better know when and where the ceremony would be'. On Monday, November 2nd, our son called and announced that 'the ceremony would be tomorrow, Tuesday, November 3rd, 4:00 p.m. at the Court House'. Although I wanted the couple to have a church wedding, I was impressed with this civil service, as the judge had a sermon and a prayer. Afterwards, we had a nice dinner at our house, complete with a little wedding cake. One of the best pictures we got was of Angela, Bobby, Melissa, and Angela's sister, Gale. I had it enlarged and mailed it to Angela's dad.   I included a letter telling him how

excited we were to have Angela and the kids in our family, and that we would look forward to meeting him when he came to visit. I tried to do all the right things to embrace my new daughter-in-law. From what I had heard, Angela's relationship with her first set of in-laws was difficult. I could understand that it would be hard for her to get to know and trust us. More than anything, I wanted her to know that we accepted her for the person she was. I asked God to in some way let me convey this to her.

The following Christmas I made Stephanie, our daughter, a coverlet for the bed in her guest room. In order to hold the quilt-like coverlet together, I machine stitched on the leaf and stems of the pattern on this fabric. Angela asked me if I had ever quilted and I said no. The truth of the matter was I had no desire whatsoever to do any quilting. Stephanie's coverlet was as close as I wanted to come to quilting! It was January 2000 when Angela told me that she had three boxes of quilt tops from her Granny, and she was wondering if I could find someone to finish them. One night we sat down and went through the boxes of quilt tops and fabric that had been stored for over 30 years. It was very obvious that she had a great love for her Granny. I had never known the love of a Grandmother. These quilt tops were made from the scraps of material left over from the clothes Granny had made for everyone. Angela pointed out the fabric that was her grandpa's pajamas, a shirt for her dad and an apron for her mother and a dress for her. I told her to pick out three tops, and I would see what I could do.

There was one that had a flower pattern made with two-inch, eight-sided pieces of material. The flowers were separated by white, eight-sided pieces. Then, there were two sections where one piece was added to the other with no pattern at all. I took this one to my friend, Karen, a quilting expert and owner of the quilt store in Winnsboro. She told me if I wanted to bring this back to the original quality, I needed to either cut off the mess at the ends or take those sections off and re-do them. To cut it off would greatly decrease the size of the quilt. I asked her if she knew anyone who could take it apart, put it back together, and quilt it. Yes, she did. Then, Karen said, "Amy, you could do this." "Forget it," I told her. I had no desire to learn to quilt. I took it back to our lake house and pondered my decision.

One of my greatest pleasures is to sit on our dock early in the morning as the sun rises over the lake. It is my prayer and quiet time. The next morning, thoughts of the quilt top entered my mind. "Dear God, should I attempt to do this quilt? Would Angela like what I would do? Would it help her to know us better, as I desired to know her?" "Lord," I prayed, "please give me your wisdom and encouragement if I am to do this." Then, I heard Karen's voice saying, "Amy, you can do this." I trusted the message God was sending my way, and I began the painstaking task of removing each little piece and saving it for the re-do. Several times, I sought Karen's advice. She was starting a quilting class and suggested that I take it. "No way, I wasn't into that." She looked at me and smiled, "Yea, right, Amy, look at what you are doing with your daughter-in-law's quilt top, and you seem to be enjoying it." I took the class.

God had opened the door of the talents he had given me that I didn't even realize I had. I really was enjoying putting my creativity to work. What a blessing, a talent for me and a gift for Angela. My goal was to give this to her for Christmas. The quilt top was done, and now, it needed to be put together and quilted. By the first of December I knew there was no way I'd have it done. Disappointed, I put it away.

Late in January 2000, Bobby called. "Mom, you and Dad are going to be grandparents in September." WOW! We never thought this would be possible and were very excited. In February, I picked up the quilt again, and instead of letting someone else quilt it, I decided to machine stitch around each of the flowers for the quilting, not realizing, how difficult and time consuming this project would become.

In April, I contacted Angela's Aunt to get the birth and death dates of Granny. I sent the aunt a picture of the quilt top and a self-addressed, stamped envelope. Within a week I had the information I needed. The following message was professionally embroidered on a separate piece of white flannel that I had stitched to the back of one corner of the quilt, trimmed in scraps of Granny's fabric.

For Angela, in Memory of Granny
Dover Pollard Ryals
Born: 11-04-1896   Died: 07-19-1980

May 6th, Angela's birthday was fast approaching. The quilt wasn't finished. Did I do the best I could? Yes, I did. Angela had no idea what I was doing or how long I had worked on this. Perhaps, even unfinished, it was time for her to know and watch the progress as I finished it. I wrapped it in white tissue paper with the corner that had the dedication turned back, so when she opened the box, that would be the first thing she would see.

Saturday, May 6, 2000, we all gathered at the Lake House to celebrate Angela's birthday. She was now five months pregnant. As she unwrapped the box, I prayed, "Please God let her like what I have done." She opened up the tissue paper and read the inscription.   "Where did you get the information about Granny?" she asked. As tears came to her eyes, she took the quilt out of the box. "Oh, this is beautiful. Thank you." By then, we all had tears of joy, and we all hugged one another. I explained to her how I got the information about Granny, and that I would continue working on the quilt until it was completed. It was a wonderful weekend and a new beginning for all of us.

On September 11, 2000, Angela gave birth to a beautiful baby boy. I finished the quilt in time to give it to her when she and Bobby brought their son, Robert Christian, home from the hospital. It now is displayed on a quilt rack in their living room.

September 2011, Angela called me the other evening wanting to know if my ears had been burning. "Well no, why do you ask?" She had been visiting her daughters-in-law and the subject of 'in laws' came up. Angela told them the quilt story and said that she had the best mother-in-law. Needless to say, it touched my heart.

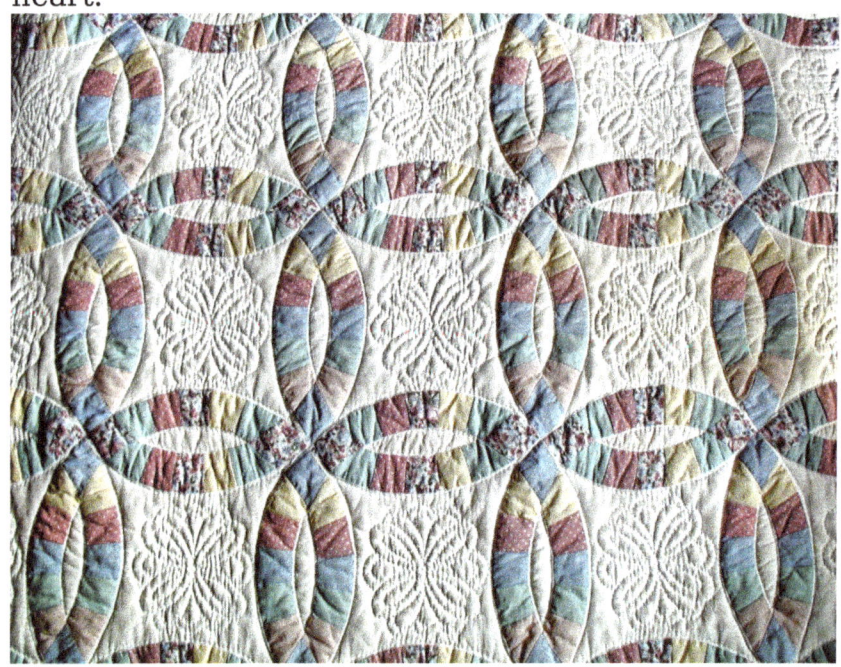

Baby Clothes

Outfit for Caleb
I may never see you wear
Except in pictures

I was talking to my girlfriend, Amy, about Caleb, when I suddenly burst into tears, and this poem was born. My first grandchild...my s o n has a son. They live far away. I have seen my grandson twice in the six months that he has graced this earth. Maybe I will see him in two months, if they come for Thanksgiving.

Bits and pieces of this precious, fleeting time are gathered like rose petals in a garden, which are too soft and pretty not to notice, gathered to grace this moment in time. God is teaching me to live in the moment. This moment is all we really have. I took my girlfriend, Candy, up on her invitation to a Bible study. A new mother was there with her infant son. I cuddled the baby. The moment was tender and peaceful.

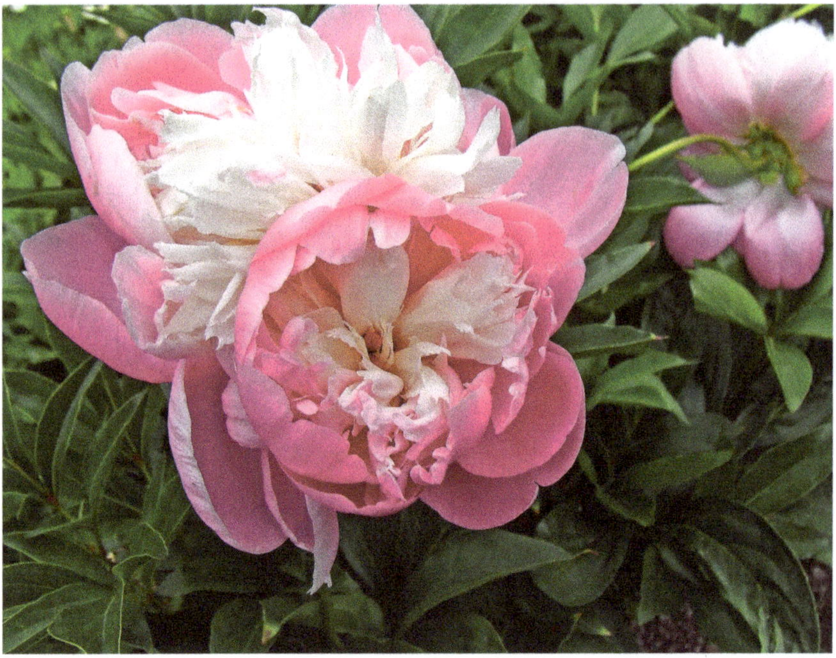

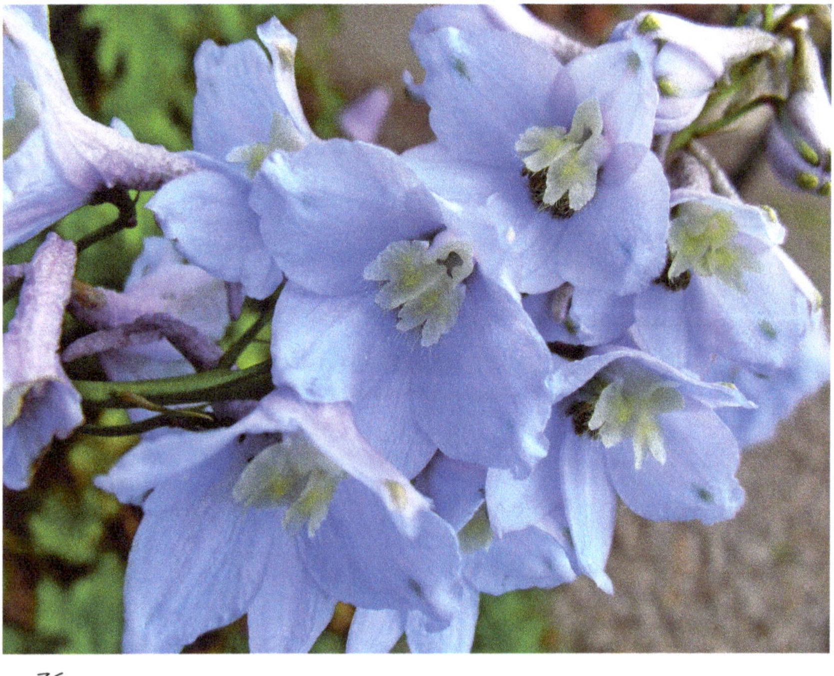

In the Garden

**A garden is a place to meditate,
To contemplate,
Perhaps a place to pray
And to soak up a bit of heaven
When we stay.**

In mid June my husband and I finally broke free from sweltering Texas in that sizzling summer of 2011 to the delightful coolness of almost 9,000 feet up in the Rocky Mountains of Lake City, Colorado. Less than 24 hours after our arrival, I found myself at Loose Arrow, the nursery just inside town. It is a garden of delights and peacefulness that draws me in, as do the mountains and stars.

Planting flowers is as much a part of me as reading, writing, hiking, and photography. It is part of my soul. Nothing could survive the Texas heat that summer, and even if it could, I had no desire to go outside to tend it or try to enjoy it.

Piled on stresses began to fade as I entered the garden. I container plant on my deck, so deer and weeds are not a problem, and I enjoy my container garden daily, as the deck is an extension of the house in this season of contentment.

There are adorable containers and precious items to help create an enchanting deck garden. I found a miniature red wagon, in celebration of my first grandchild! Directly from a fairy tale, I see a frog wearing a golden crown. I am smitten with a tiny, blue chair that will perfectly hold a small, red flower pot I have. Gathering moss covered rocks, and uncovering pine cones will be a fun addition as well as the small, decorative, bird houses from the basement shelves and other treasures yet to be discovered.

I will dig up some sweet-smelling mint, growing by the river on our property. I felt a smile loosen my shoulders. I began to breathe the clean mountain air and fragrant garden. Joyful ideas were flowing. I had all day to be enveloped in flowers and create my magical garden.

I went to pay. In my haste I didn't even check to see if I had money. Up here I am far away from places that regularly take credit cards. It was not Patti, the owner, who was there that day, yet trust overflows. Taffy told me to go ahead and take my flowers and things and pay when I returned. I was in the garden. I was far away from many stresses. Patti and Taffy are my garden girlfriends. God's a little closer in a garden.

A Park

The commons, a square
Colors flair autumn in air
God and man sit down

What is Truthfully Gold

Not extremely hard to define
Though we can misinterpret the sign
At the start what is perhaps a joy
Later too often becomes a ploy
As day goes towards night
The lesson can be discerned without fright.

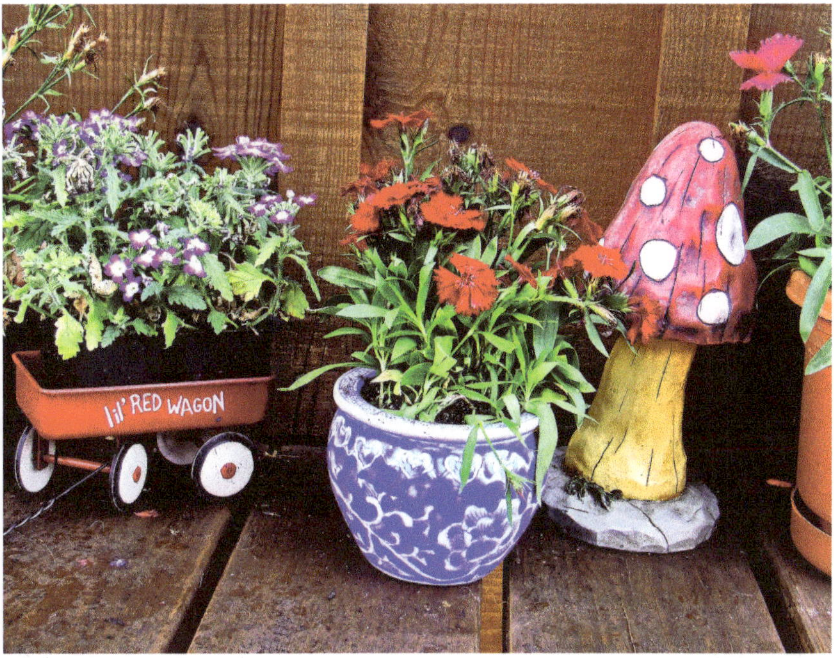
lil' RED WAGON

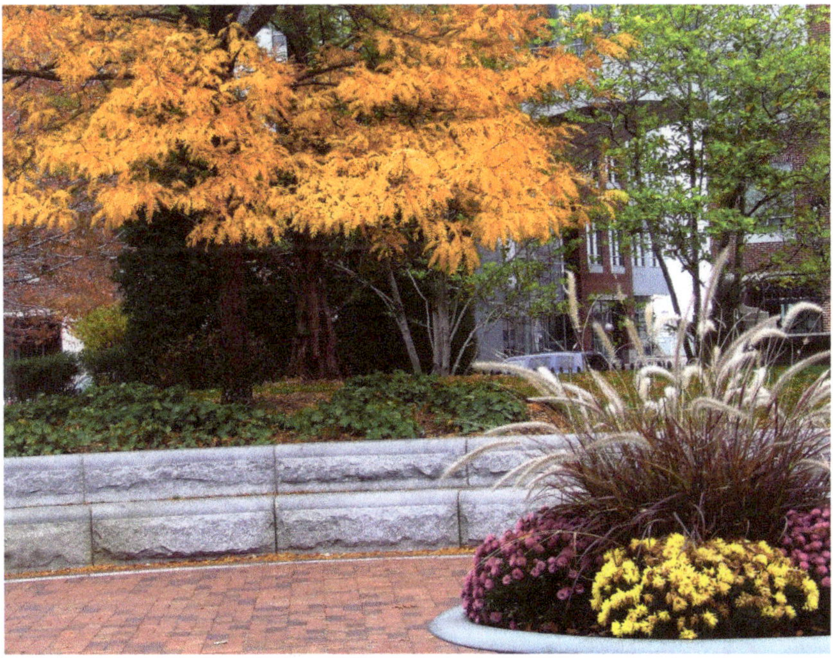

Amy

Due to the merger of Trans World Airlines into American Airlines, the summer of 2001 was a roller coaster ride for the employees of TWA. Will we get interviews, get jobs with AA, or be out of work? Stephanie and I had a trip planned to our long, loved spot in the world, Lake City, Colorado.

We made a jeep trip to American Basin where Stephie wanted to hike. I had no desire to hike; instead I sat by the stream, enjoying nature. Another woman drove up, and let her children out to go hiking. We started chatting. I told her the concerns I had for the future. She had been attending a Bible Retreat and shared the following verse with me... Isaiah 46 verses 3 and 4 which says, "Listen to me, all you that I have upheld since you were conceived, and have carried you since your birth. Even to your old age and gray hairs I am he, I am he who will sustain you. I have made you and I will carry you; I will sustain you and I will rescue you." That verse has given me peace.

Whenever I become anxious, I remember... even to your old age and gray hairs, I am he who will sustain you.

This was given to me, as woman to woman, we connected that August day in 2001.

Julie

Girlfriends like to meet for lunch or serve dessert with **tea and talk**. We love to exchange recipes.

Easy and delicious quiche recipe: ingredients for one, (easily doubled).
- Unbaked deep dish pie crust
- 3 eggs
- Swiss cheese (whatever you like; I use low fat)
- 2 T flour
- Salt (I like garlic salt) and pepper to taste
- 1 cup of low fat half and half
- Frozen spinach or cooked broccoli, enough to cover the bottom of the pie crust. If you want meat, cooked ham or chicken can be used or served on the side.
- Grated, extra sharp cheddar cheese (enough to cover the top of the pie crust)

Preheat oven to 350. Cover the bottom of pie crust with Swiss or whatever, add veggies, mix well the eggs, half and half, salt and pepper and flour and pour over cheese in pie crust and cover with grated, extra sharp cheddar cheese (enough to cover the top of the pie crust) and bake at 350 for about an hour. It's done when a sharp knife comes out clean in the center.

Fresh sliced tomatoes are tasty on the side. They are nutritious and pretty, as well.

I gave this recipe to Amy who prepared and enjoyed it many times. One day she called to tell me that she prepared it that afternoon, but forgot the eggs! "Amy! HOW could you forget the eggs!? It's quiche for goodness sake! Eggs are the main part of the recipe!"

Yeah, not terribly long afterwards I had to eat humble pie. "Amy, I made the quiche recipe, and...I...forgot to put the eggs in...it is different that way."

She laughed...and laughed.

The BEST chocolates cake

I made this VERY Easy and extremely delicious chocolate cake recipe for the first time when I was visiting Amy's lake home in Texas, also for the first time, appropriately enough. **Warning!** Prepare this only when you are having people over so there are no leftovers ~ it is seriously addictive:

- 1 box yellow, moist cake mix
- 1 small & 1 large box chocolate pudding mix
- 4 eggs, room temperature
- 1 cup oil
- ½ cup Kahlua
- ½ cup vodka
- 1 container store bought fudge icing

Preheat oven 350

In mixer bowl combine the cake mix, pudding mixes, and eggs. Mix until creamy then add oil, Kahlua and vodka. Twirl until there are no lumps. Pour into an 8 cup, well oiled bunt pan and bake for about 45 minutes; test doneness with a toothpick or knife in the center. Let the cake sit one minute, then invert pan onto a plate and ice cake while hot, allowing icing to melt into the cake.

This sensational recipe came from the laugh-out-loud book, *Being Dead is No Excuse*, by Gyden Metcalfe and Charlotte Hays.

SPINACH SALAD – From my girlfriend Susie: Colorful, fun and easy, delicious and healthy!
- Baby spinach
- Shredded carrots
- Shredded purple cabbage
- White mushrooms, sliced
- Craisins, sprinkle on top
- Almonds, toasted, sprinkle on top
- Blue cheese crumbles, sprinkle on top

Mix amount needed of each ingredient. Use favorite balsamic vinaigrette or French Catalina dressing. We like a slightly sweetened balsamic.

Bake 350 for about 15 minutes – check often – until crispy, crunchy but not burnt. I like to eat them hot out of the oven

VERY EASY BARBEQUE CHICKEN
    Early in the morning, place in the crock pot frozen chicken, and then cover with your favorite barbeque sauce, set it on low all day.

VERY EASY PEANUT BUTTER COOKIES
- 1 C peanut butter
- 1 C sugar (I use somewhat less)
- 1 egg

Bake 350 for about 11 min.

SUNDAY CHICKEN

My girlfriend Roxie and I had our children about the same time when our family lived in Tulsa. We have been through and shared a lot over the years. Thank you, Roxie, for sharing your Sunday recipe!

- 8-10 Chicken tenders not breaded
- 1 cup uncooked rice
- 1 can cream of chicken soup
- 1 can of Milk
- ½ cup water

Put rice in baking dish, layer chicken tenders on rice, pour cream of chicken mixture on top. Bake 350 for 30 to 40 minutes

This is simple for the kids to do. They would get on a chair, take the measuring cup, scoop the rice up, make it level, then pour into the baking dish. They would layer the frozen chicken tenders on the rice. Then, in a small bowl, the kids would mix the cream of chicken soup with the milk, water, and pour over the rice and chicken.

We set the timer on the oven, then off to church we go. When we came home and pull into the garage, we could smell Sunday Dinner. We were so busy during the week with school and sports etc...

WE ALWAYS ATE SUNDAY DINNER AT HOME!!!

FROZEN BANANA TREAT TASTES LIKE ICE-CREAM

Here's another way to use very ripe bananas other than banana bread. Slice very ripe bananas and freeze. When completely frozen, put the bananas in a food processor and purée until the bananas are the consistency of ice cream. Enjoy! I have added ingredients such as: wheat germ, cinnamon, vanilla but the beauty of this treat is the simplicity!

MARGARET'S RECIPE FOR ANGEL BISCUIT DOUGH
- 1 pkg dry yeast
- 1 teaspoon salt
- 1/2 cup warm water
- 1 teaspoon baking soda
- 2 Cups buttermilk
- 3 Tablespoon sugar
- 5 cups flour
- 3/4 cup vegetable shortening
- 3 teaspoons baking powder

Dissolve the yeast in warm water. Add to buttermilk. Sift dry ingredients two times into a large bowl. Cut in Shortening. Add buttermilk and yeast mixture. Work dough only until well moistened. Cover and refrigerate to use as needed.

To use, remove desired amount. Roll 3/4 inch thick and cut. Place on greased cookie sheet and let stand 5 minutes. Bake at 400 degrees until nicely browned, about 12 minutes.

Margaret gave me this recipe, but it also appears in her book, *Who in the World is Margaret Sherman?* I hadn't picked up her book in a long time. When I thought about a couple of recipes for **Tea and Talk**, Margaret's name came into my head. We had talked on the phone many times. Even though, we had only spent 2 or 3 afternoons together, it was a friendship that had its impact on my life.

She was as tall as I am short, smart, witty, always positive, giving the most of herself, bringing out the best in everyone she met. Our relationships with other women can be short or enduring. It is the meaningful memories that warm our hearts and encourage our endeavors. Women do this best. Margaret Sherman did this for me.

CHOCOLATE SHEET CAKE

- 2 c sugar
- ½ c Crisco
- 2 c flour
- 1 c water
- ½ tsp salt
- 4 Tbsp cocoa
- 1 stick margarine
- ½ c buttermilk
- 2 eggs beaten
- 1 tsp vanilla
- 1 tsp soda
- 1 tsp cinnamon

ICING
- 2 tsp vanilla
- 6 Tbsp milk
- 1 stick margarine
- 1 c chopped nuts
- 4 Tbsp cocoa
- 1 box powder sugar

Sift flour, sugar and salt together in mixing bowl. Set aside and bring to rapid boil, margarine, Crisco, cocoa, and water. Pour over flour and sugar. Mix well and add buttermilk, beaten eggs, soda, vanilla and cinnamon. Pour into greased and floured sheet cake pan, 11 x 16 inches, and bake in 350 degree oven for about 20 minutes. Make icing and have ready to spread on cake when removed from oven. Cool and cut into squares.

Icing: Bring all ingredients except sugar to a rapid boil and pour over the sugar. I bring the ingredients to a boil, and then put the sugar in the pot, and I think it takes more than a box of sugar. I also have to use my electric mixer to beat the sugar to make it smooth.

We were all sitting around the table about to have dessert, when my ten year old grandson, Robert, asked me why we always had chocolate sheet cake.
"The last time you were here, about three weeks ago, your Dad asked for it. Today your Aunt Stephie is here, and she asked for it." He pondered that for a minute and then in his ultimate wisdom, he said, "Well grandma, I think it is time we moved on."

There are so many times in life that it is time for us "to move on." I have shared this story with many of my friends, who are trying to made decisions. Every one of us will reach the point where we have to give up the old and start the new, as it is "a time for us to move on."

Acknowledgments

Amy

I would like to acknowledge and give thanks to Dr. Lillian Soloman, Dr. Janet Ragsdale, and to the woman I called my other mother, Phyllis Townsend.

To my life time friend, Phyllis Kayne, whose support is never ending, and Dava Poli, whose encouragement has always been there for me. With Julie Stephens, my friend of great depth, **Tea and Talk** has become a reality…thank you, my dear friend.

Julie

Thank you to my husband, always, for your support and help. Thank you Susie Wheaton. Thank you for always being ready, willing, and able to edit.

Thank you, especially, to Stephanie Pierson for letting her very personal story be told. I have faith that it is an inspiration to others. Thank you Olyve Abbott. Thank you for your sharing spirit and eagle eye.

I have been blessed that so many girlfriends have touched my life. Always it has been at some vital transitioning time…college, teaching, theater involvement, moving to a new community, becoming a first time mother, making play dates with our growing children, developing closer relationships with female relatives, and we girlfriends were as close as is possible, but that time has passed, and we are now only in each others memories. With other girlfriends we still connect every once in awhile through cards and emails or phone now and then. Still others will continue to be tightly joined together in the course of the month or week; some of us will forever meet for **Tea & Talk**. Thank you to all my girlfriends.

About the authors

Amy Pierson is a retired airline administer and the creator of "Amy's Quilted Decor and More" featuring Oat Pillows. Her poetry has been published in "The international WHO'S WHO in Poetry" and her latest poem is in the book "From a Window Looking Out." While being an enthusiastic quilter, she also dabbles in watercolor painting. In her second year at Michigan State University, she met and married her husband, Bob and they have two children, a daughter - in-law, and three grandchildren.

Julie Stephens is a certified teacher with a master's in education, a BFA in theater and is an award winning photographer. Julie's first book, *Reflections In The San Juan Mountains* is in its second printing. Julie and her husband, Bruce, have been married for 34 years and treasure living in nature with an active lifestyle of hiking and bicycling. The Stephens are the proud parents of a grown son and daughter and became first time grandparents when Caleb Bruce Stephens was born in March 2011.

About the photographs

P.8 – Taken in August 2010 on one of Amy and Julie's outings together in Crested Butte, Colorado, along a colorful lane of shops and restaurants.

P.15 – Celtic Cross from the Aran Islands, Ireland.

P.17 – The wildflower picture was taken in the summer time in the country in Whitt, Texas. Whitt is fifteen minutes from Mineral Wells, a half hour from Weatherford, an hour from Fort Worth, and if you still have no idea, don't be concerned.

P.21 – The nest of robin's eggs was taken in Lake City, Colorado in a wilderness preserve area near our mountain home in the summer of 2011. The hummingbird was taken out of our window, the same year.

P.23 – The 9/11 memorial taken at Jones Beach Island which is a barrier island linked to Long Island, New York on October 2010. Jones Beach faces the Atlantic Ocean and is a popular beach on the east coast.

P.31 – The peach poppy was taken in the summer 2009 in the Secret Garden on Silver Street, in Lake City, Colorado. Brenda Wagner is the caretaker for this little treasure.

P.32 – Red Mountain Lake City, Colorado, across from Lake San Cristobal. The bread is from Howth, Ireland, a side trip when my husband and I visited our son and his wife when they were living in Dublin in the autumn of 2009. Howth with its surrounding rural district is now a busy suburb of Dublin.

P.40 – "The Fly Fisherman's Dream," is a carving created by Amy's husband, Bob, who specializes in wildlife subjects. *Wildlife In Wood* by Bob Pierson.

P.42 – A wild rose found on a walk near Lake City, Colorado.

P.44 – The tree with tire swing was taken November 2010 in Newton, a suburb of Boston, while visiting my daughter.
Crystal Peak, near Lake City, Colorado, was taken from our deck one summer evening. More often than not, Crystal is a stunning, inspirational backdrop for colorful summer sunsets.
P.51 – A beautiful wall hanging created by Amy. P.53 – The American Basin in the San Juan Mountains, the wild flowers are breathtaking, such as the Colorado State flower, the Columbine.
P.54 – Aran Island, Ireland, from the Fort of Dun Aegean, a semi-circle stone fort that is safeguarded on its open side by cliffs. The fort has endured since 2000 BC. There are few moments of travel as halting as taking in the Atlantic Ocean over the edge of a 4000 year-old fort.
P.56 – My husband and I were visiting our daughter in Brownsville, Texas when we happened upon the annual sandcastle building contest on South Padre Island, near Port Isabel.
P.64 – A beautiful gate is all that remains from an ancient monastery on the Aran Islands, Ireland. The second picture is also from Ireland. My daughter-in-law and I were walking together when she saw the black face lamb turn towards us and I finally got my picture!
P.66 – The tree was taken at Glendalough (Glen of Two Lakes), Ireland. This is a beautiful area that once was a monastic settlement, founded in the 6th century by Saint Kevin, a hermit priest.
P.68 – A quaint cottage in Ireland. The second picture is from Deer Lakes, a campground in Gunnison National Forest, Colorado, on a stunning autumn day in September 2009.

The Creation of Adam (detail) Michelangelo (1475-1564)

Additional copies of
Tea and Talk with Friends
can be obtained from
handsbestrong.com

Questions or comments about this material can be directed to: support@handsbestrong.com

May the graciousness of the LORD our God be upon us;
    prosper the work of our hands;
        prosper our handiwork.   Psalm 90:17

www.ingramcontent.com/pod-product-compliance
Lightning Source LLC
Chambersburg PA
CBHW062113290426
44110CB00023B/2796